How wonderful it is...

HAVING FRIENDS IN OUR LIVES

WRITTEN & ILLUSTRATED BY

Susan Squellati Florence

A HELEN EXLEY GIFTBOOK

This book is written in thanksgiving to all friends. To each and every one who is a friend to someone. Like fields of wildflowers, you surprise us with unexpected joy. You remind us that life is beautiful. In this world of show and pretense you give us something real, something timeless... your friendship.

We all need friends. They make us happy. Friends can turn our tears into laughter. They give us the special feeling of being connected and close to others... instead of feeling alone.

They let us know that we matter... that our lives make a difference... just by their caring.

Friends are the ones we want to talk to, we need to talk to. We share our life journeys with them. Friends understand us... and accept us. Friends help us without our asking and heal us by just being there. We feel better about ourselves when we are with a friend. How wonderful it is to have friends!

Like a field of wildflowers
friends surprise us
with unexpected joy.

With friends
we share unpressured space.
There are no judgements
or expectations of us
to be anyone else
than who we are.

When we are with a friend
we can be
our own unique self.

When we are with a friend
we can talk about what matters.

We can dream our dreams
admit our doubts,
reveal our fears
and not be afraid to hope out loud.

A friend sees our dreams
coming true,
and helps us
believe in ourself.

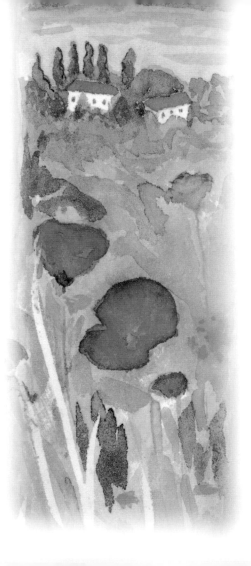

A friend can't solve our problems
fix our relationships,
or make our decisions...
but a friend can listen
and somehow
everything is lighter.

We feel better about ourself
by just being with a friend.

We are able to grow freely
in the open, loving spaces
of friendship.

Friends give us the freedom
to express ourself...
to dance
and be silly
and sing until dawn.
The freedom to be ugly
and moody and weak.
We can eat too much ice cream
and chocolate
and celebrate everything...
or just do nothing.

It's all okay
with a friend.

*With our friend we can share
the world within ourself.*

It is a welcome relief to talk to our friend
after a hectic day.
It is healing to talk to our friend
after a depressing day.

*Friends help us
open our hearts
and deepen our spirits.*

As we talk to a friend .
we can listen to ourself
and learn more
about who we are.

We can be true to ourself
when we are with a friend.

Our friend can share with us
our silence.

We thrive and grow
in the company of friends...
because we are loved.

In friendship
we take time to share
and celebrate the joy
of each other's lives.

*In friendship
we live our lives
more fully, more openly
more deeply.*

We smile more.

Our friend reminds us
that life is beautiful.

Like spring coming to our lives
our friends renew us.

Like a field of wildflowers,
friends bring us abundant happiness.

If we have friends
along the journey of our life,
no matter what life brings,
we will move forward
with laughter, grace
and love.

*How wonderful it is
my friend,
to have you in my life.*

ABOUT THE AUTHOR

Susan Squellati Florence

The well loved and collected greeting cards of Susan Florence have sold hundreds of millions of copies in the last three decades. Her giftbooks have sold over one and a half million copies.

With words of gentle wisdom and original paintings, Susan Florence brings her unique style to all her gift products and her readers have written time and again to thank her and tell her how the books were a profound help to them. People have told Susan that her words speak to them of what they cannot say... but what they feel.

Susan Florence's completely new collection of giftbooks in **The Journeys Series** invites the readers to pause and look deeply into their lives. "We all need more time to rediscover and reflect on what is meaningful and important in our own *lives... and what brings us joy and beauty. Writing these books in* The Journeys Series *has helped me understand more fully the value of love and acceptance in helping us through the difficult times as we journey through life."*

Susan lives with her husband, Jim, in Ojai, California. They have two grown children, Brent and Emily.

THE JOURNEYS SERIES